David Huerta

POEMS
POEMAS

poetry translation centre

First published in 2010
by The Poetry Translation Centre Ltd
PO Box 61051
London SE16 4YY

www.poetrytranslation.org

Poems © David Huerta, 2010
Translations © Jamie McKendrick
Introduction © Tom Boll

ISBN: 978-0-9560576-2-4

The Poetry Translation Centre gratefully acknowledges the financial
support of Arts Council England.

British Library Cataloguing-in-Publication Data.
A catalogue record for this book is available from the British Library.

Designed in Albertina by Libanus Press
and printed in Great Britain by the
MPG Books Group, Bodmin and King's Lynn

Contents

Introduction	4
Poem by Gottfried Benn	7
Thirteen Attempts on the Life of Trivial Love	9
Open and Shut	15
Prayer	17
Aural	19
Heaven's Kitchen	21
Entropy in Wiesbaden	23
Spell for September	25
The Child is Father of the Man	27

Introduction

David Huerta was born in Mexico City in 1949. He grew up during a transitional period of Mexican history. The hopes of the political left, which had been animated by the Cuban Revolution, would appear increasingly beleaguered as the 1960s progressed, and the ensuing decade brought a series of repressive dictatorships across Latin America. Huerta himself witnessed the *Matanza de Tlatelolco* (Tlatelolco Massacre) of 1968 when government forces opened fire on student demonstrators in Mexico City.

Yet this period also introduced young Mexicans to a wave of new philosophical ideas from continental Europe. In particular, it brought a fascination with the ways that language encroaches on the interactions between self and world. That awareness of language is always present in Huerta's poems, whether as explicit reflection or, more commonly, as a taste for extended metaphorical excursions. In 'Prayer', the speaker calls for the preservation of a moment 'here now among us': 'it casts its yellow light and swells / like the sun or like flaming lemons / – and tastes of the sea, of loved hands / and smells like a street in Paris / where we were happy.' What begins as an unremarkable call for mindfulness of the present launches into a figurative journey that engages the senses (sight, taste and smell) and startling shifts of imaginative scale (sun to lemons to sea to street). Yet the very expansiveness of this language suggests that the experience has never quite been captured. Indeed, the present moment gives way to 'a street in Paris', a fleeting memory of the past, and a recognition that the preservation of the here and now is a precarious endeavour.

Huerta's poems can be colloquial, fanciful, and dense in turns, but they are linked by a strong dramatic portrait of a speaker trying to orient himself in shifting landscapes of word and world, memory and desire. There is a consistently intimate note to poems which are often addressed directly to a lover. While the meditative cast of his work precludes direct confession, a number of the poems here betray an autobiographical inspiration: whether the difficult feelings about masculinity of 'Thirteen Attempts on the Life of Trivial Love'; or the more casual anecdote of 'Aural'; or the exchange between present and past selves of 'The Child is Father of the Man'. Even in works that refer to other poets, such as 'Poem by Gottfried Benn', the encounter is framed in terms of a troubling personal narrative: 'But how they stayed here those images the ghosts / of those lacerating images is something I must / come to terms with it won't be easy but I have to do it.' This passage is a pointed reminder that the frequently baroque expansiveness of Huerta's imagery is not mere ornament. Poetic language is here a visceral experience.

It is now nearly forty years since David Huerta published his first collection of verse, *El jardín de la luz* (The Garden of Light) (1972). We have chosen to concentrate on his later poems, from *Historia* (History) (1990), *Desdoblamientos* (Doubling) (1997), *La música de lo que pasa* (The Music of What Happens) (1997), and *La calle blanca* (The White Street) (2006). His novel-length *Incurable* (Incurable) (1987) is a remarkable document but it did not lend itself to selection in a modest volume such as we offer here. Huerta's poems, which themselves deal with the translation of an evasive experience into words, confront the translator with particular challenges. Jamie McKendrick has managed to capture both the physical precision and the imaginative flight of Huerta's world. He presents a poet with an eye for the mundane as well as the erudite; a speaker intent on rescuing meaning from the fluid motions of a passing world.

TOM BOLL

Translator's Note

I am deeply indebted to Tom Boll for his encouragement and expert vigilance throughout, and also to Xon de Ros and Erica Segre for their help and advice.

POEMA DE GOTTFRIED BENN

Tenía que irme pero un poema de Gottfried Benn
me detuvo en el arranque de ese impulso
no saben ustedes qué poema terrible

Una flor se deshacía en medio de una autopsia
y el doctor que había abierto el cadáver
veía cómo los pétalos se atoraban en las vísceras

También los guantes del médico se llenaban
de pétalos y de sanguaza era todo impresionante
pero sólo era un poema y yo tenía que irme

No sé si me fui pero las imágenes de ese poema
de Gottfried Benn –por lo demás una figura
no muy simpática– no se fueron se quedaron aquí

Cómo se quedaron aquí esas imágenes las huellas
de esas figuras desgarradas es algo que deberé
investigar no será fácil lo sé pero debo hacerlo

POEM BY GOTTFRIED BENN

I had to go out but a poem by Gottfried Benn
stopped me in my tracks – you've no idea
quite how disturbing that poem was

A flower fell apart in the middle of an autopsy
and the doctor who'd cut open the corpse
saw how those petals landed among the inner organs

Even the medic's rubber gloves were covered
with petals and blood it was utterly breathtaking
but only a poem and I had to go out

I'm not sure if I left but the images
of that poem by Benn – frankly not
a very appealing figure – never left they stayed here

But how they stayed here those images the ghosts
of those lacerating images is something I must
come to terms with it won't be easy but I have to do it

TRECE INTENCIONES CONTRA EL AMOR TRIVIAL

Si la palabra es el principio de la acción, liberemos la palabra de la esclavitud doméstica rellenándola de cáncer, del virus más venenoso e incurable, y lancémosla al cuerpo del amor trivial.
LLUÍS FERNÁNDEZ, *El anarquista desnudo*

1. Razones viudas por las que
"sucede que me canso de ser hombre",
líquido desflecado y fértil
de la mujer que no soy; líquido
terso, cristalino, que sale
de los senos que no tengo.

2. Enigmas, siempre, del coito
conmigo mismo: uróboro,
Anillo de Moebius. Evidencias
de una manada, de una multitud
que se difunde dentro de mí
–circula, quiere algo: ama, se ama.

3. Hay mujeres, mal sueño mío,
muertas en mí –arrojadas como cabelleras.

4. En mis fotografías de niño estoy
indiferenciado, un amasijo
de palpitante energía carnal, sin
sonrisa, sin miedo, sin neurosis.

5. Misterios de mis labios bajo el bigote
imperioso y solipsista, hirsuto paisaje
de los caracteres secundarios.

THIRTEEN ATTEMPTS ON THE LIFE OF TRIVIAL LOVE

If the word is the basis for action, let's deliver the word from its domestic servitude, infecting it with cancer, with the most venomous and incurable virus, and hurl it at the body of trivial love.
LLUÍS FERNÁNDEZ, *The Naked Anarchist*

1. Widowed reasons why
'it happens that I'm tired of being a man',
torn fertile liquid
of the woman I'm not; clear
liquid overflowing from
the breasts I don't possess.

2. Always the enigmas of coitus
conducted with myself: uroboros,
Möbius strip. Evidence left
by a handful, a mob
that spreads within me
– circulates, wants something: loves, loves itself.

3. There are women, nightmares of mine,
dead inside me – discarded like scalps.

4. In the photographs of me as a child
I pale into the background, a tangle
of trembling carnal energy, without
smiles, without fear, without neurosis.

5. Mysteries of my lips under that
imperious solipsistic moustache,
the hirsute landscape of minor characters.

6. Tacto y sudor, míos, de hombre,
a veces, sobre una carne en penumbra
deleitada, carne desconocida, sedienta;
carne imborrable, con un corazón
afilado y leve, y otros latidos milenarios,
caudalosa carne abrazada a mí, a mis
ficciones concretas de persona, mi yo turbio.

7. Una sequía nos divide,
mi vertebral llamarada
y tus ansiosas vértebras
lo saben interminablemente.

8. ¡Ah!, instantáneos abismos
de mi apetito, la mayoría de edad
y sus frustrados paraísos, los jardines
parásitos del hambre individualista
que va sintiendo el cráneo macho,
secamente, resplandeciendo por lo bajo
y con los dientes apretados.

9. Falo y esperma, grandes símbolos
y minuciosos abalorios del amor trivial
—losa diamantina en mis lomos adultos.

10. Pero quién quiere culpas, por lo demás:
pedazos muertos del falo-gimnoto,
pedazos muertos de la vulva-caverna: Culpas.

11. No quiero culpas prendidas,
como millar de escapularios,
en el envés de mi falda de hombre.

6. The sense of touch, sweat, my own, a man's,
at times, over flesh in joyous half-light,
unknown, thirsting flesh; unforgettable flesh
with a heart sharpened and made buoyant
and other ancient heartbeats, generous flesh
cleaving to me, to my embodied fictions
of someone else, of my own shady self.

7. A drought divides us,
both the flame of my spine
and your fiery vertebrae
know it forever.

8. Ah! Sudden chasms opening
in my appetite: coming of age
and its frustrated heavens, the gardens
of such predatory hunger
that the male skull,
dramatically underlit,
senses with gritted teeth.

9. Phallus and sperm, towering symbols
and meticulous trinkets of trivial love –
adamantine tombstone in my adult loins.

10. And yet who wants this guilt anyway:
dead fragments of the gimno-phallus,
of the vulva-cave: Guilt.

11. I don't want these rooted guilts,
like countless devotional scapulars
hung inside, the wrong side, of my manly robe.

12. Doy mi palabra de hombre y cuánto pesa,
circula austera, devuelve un aroma
musculado y gentil, de cedo-el-paso, de ir
por el lado de afuera en la banqueta, de
extender una mano —sólo tendones, venas.

13. Mis palabras quisieran
restañar esa herida: la
mordedura del amor trivial.

Amor, amor, detén tu planta impura.
VICENTE ALEIXANDRE

12. I give my man's word – how much it weighs,
severely circulates, distilling the gentle,
muscular scent of giving way, of stepping out
to the pavement's edge, of stretching forth
a hand – merely tendons, veins.

13. My words would like to
heal this wound: bitten
deep by trivial love.

Love, love, stay your impure stride.
VICENTE ALEIXANDRE

ABRES Y CIERRAS

Abres un filo de navaja
para que gotee la transparencia.

Cierras el sonámbulo cubo de la noche
y un río de sombra se derrama.

Abres y cierras el diafragma líquido
de mi corazón –y amanezco

en el decuplicado y lento
destello de tus manos.

OPEN AND SHUT

You open the blade of a flick knife
so it drips transparency.

You shut the restless cube of night
and a stream of shadow ramifies.

You open and shut the liquid diaphragm
of my heart – and at dawn I arrive

in the stately, tenfold
starlight of your hands.

PLEGARIA

Señor, salva este momento.
Nada tiene de prodigio o milagro
como no sea una sospecha
de inmortalidad, un aliento
de salvación. Se parece
a tantos otros momentos...
Pero está aquí entre nosotros
y crece como una luz amarilla
de sol y de encendidos limones
—y sabe a mar, a manos amadas,
huele como una calle de París
donde fuimos felices. Sálvalo
en la memoria o rescátalo
para la luz que declina
sobre esta página,
aunque apenas la toque.

PRAYER

Lord, save this moment.
There's nothing outlandish or
miraculous about it, unless it holds
a hint of immortality, a breath
of salvation. It looks like
any number of other moments . . .
But it's here now among us:
it casts its yellow light and swells
like the sun or like flaming lemons
– and tastes of the sea, of loved hands
and smells like a street in Paris
where we were happy. Save it
in your memory or deliver it
into the light that sets
on this page,
barely touching it.

AURAL

Escarcha sucia del *audio*
en la penumbra nómada
del automóvil;
ciénaga de sonidos
en donde la aguja del oído
apenas puede moverse.
De pronto, una *torch singer*
desmenuza a Wittgenstein
con tenedores de Cante...
¿Cómo lo hace? ¿Cómo
desenlaza, destraba los lenguajes,
hace fluir el mundo –y por añadidura
suma la gracia
y la tragedia?
El automóvil
entra en la noche
ungido por la música.

AURAL

Gritty frost from
the radio speaker
in the car's
nomadic shadows:
a swamp of sounds
in which hearing's
needle can
barely move.
Out of nowhere,
a torch singer
slices through Wittgenstein
with the cutlery
of *cante jondo* . . .
How does she do it? –
unstitch, unseam
language itself,
make the world flow and
if that wasn't enough
hit the twin peaks
of grace and tragedy?
The car
anointed with music
slips into the night.

COCINA DEL PARAÍSO

Había utensilios infernales en la cocina del Paraíso,
ollas dobladas de color violáceo,
hinchados tenedores en cuyos pliegues
se ensartaban saliva de arcángeles y voces deshilachadas
que provenían de la camisa izquierda de Dios.

Una sopa fue preparándose y apareció el Amor,
un caldo peregrino adornado con inflamadas escrituras
y reflejos de playa en vacaciones. El aceite se hizo fuego,
entró en los cuerpos y luego se encajó, activo, iridiscente,
en los ojos de los bienaventurados.

El aquelarre barroco se detuvo: longitudinales olores
invadieron la cocina paradisiaca,
limpios condimentos para el edificio febril
de la primavera y sus ondulaciones, abriles
de dientes florales, mandíbulas llenas de libélulas,
todo el ropaje de Eros para la Ensalada
y sus rizos, el esplendor de los acuchillados abrazos
y el mar de las manos, todo azul y multiplicándose.

HEAVEN'S KITCHEN

Heaven's kitchen is supplied with infernal utensils,
sagging, lilac-coloured cauldrons, fat forks
between whose prongs are tangled strings
of archangels' spit and frayed voices
that rose from the left-hand shirt of God.

A soup was being cooked when Love appeared,
a rare broth sprinkled with flaming scriptures
and glints of seaside holidays. The oil became fire,
seeped into the skin and stayed, vigorous,
iridescent, in the eyes of the blessed.

The elaborate coven stopped work: elongated odours
invaded the heavenly kitchen; pure spices
for the feverish construction of Spring
and its rippling; Aprils whose flowers are teeth,
whose jaws are crammed with dragonflies;
Eros's entire wardrobe for the Salad
with its curled coiffure; the brilliance of stabbed embraces
and the sea of hands, blue as can be, multiplying.

ENTROPÍA EN WIESBADEN

Por el romano muro te asomaste
a ver la calle alemana
bajo la lluvia tenaz y declinanate.
Lo que viste fue el bullicio, la fractal
escritura del desgaste europeo.
Mucho dinero, finas ropas,
edificios cuidadosos, gestos agrios,
mala comida– Goethe, en fin,
en su áulico, nemoroso
y patriarcal papel de santo doctus, poeta
enciclopédico.
Nada que contar de regreso,
nada sino la lluvia ahora pertinaz
y final. Un soplo del Espíritu Santo
entraba por la boca de los minutos–
pero tú, presente, más cuidadosa
que las Edades Medias
de la Selva Negra,
atestiguabas el sermón puritano
y el sedimento postindustrial,
las palabras eclipsantes
de cualquier académico, los consejos
de algún editor
despistado in Francfort. La entropía
se apoderaba de Wiesbaden
y tú renacías incesante
contra el fulgor del tiempo.

ENTROPY IN WIESBADEN

You peeped out over the Roman wall
into the German street
battered by the slant, stubborn rain.
What you saw was Europe worn away,
its crowded, fractal script.
Lots of money, well-cut clothes,
prim dwellings, curt gestures,
ghastly food – and, finally Goethe
in his memorious, courtier mode,
patriarch, *santo doctus*, mode
of the all-enlightened poet.
Nothing to tell on your return
except for the now constant,
final rain. A breath of the Holy Spirit
entered the mouth of the passing moment –
but you, present, more diligent
with detail than the Middle Ages
of the Black Forest,
bore witness to the puritan sermon
and the post-industrial dust,
the overbearing views of
some academic, the counsel
of an editor astray
in Frankfurt. Entropy
engulfed Wiesbaden
while over and over you were reborn
against the blaze of time.

CONJURO DESDE SEPTIEMBRE

Fuego verde, niebla en el aire . . .
[. . .]
En una hora, en media hora, para que se vaya como una niebla,
que se vaya como una mariposa . . .
Rezo tzotzil para curar la epilepsia

Que la mano se abra hacia el espejo del sueño
Que el ojo se cierre hacia el manojo de los nervios
Que la espalda se suavice en el reposo cristalino
Que la boca se distienda bajo la electricidad de la noche
Que el cuello se afloje en la flor del reposo
Que la nariz se eleve en el perfume blanco del día
Que la pierna se alargue detrás del magnetismo del viaje
Que el pubis se encienda en el terciopelo del abrazo
Que la cadera se curve en el esplendor de la brisa
Que la oreja se despierte bajo el tintineo del contacto
Que el pelo se derrame desde el muro del cráneo
Que el pecho se ilumine entre las astillas del grito
Que el hombro se duerma ante la huella del neblí
Que el pie se extravíe entre las magias del tiempo
Que la garganta se oscurezca con la sílaba del espacio

SPELL FOR SEPTEMBER

Green fire, fog in the air
[. . .]
In an hour, a half-hour, let it disperse like the fog,
let it fly off like a butterfly.
Tzotzil prayer to cure epilepsy

Let the hand open to the mirror world of dreams
Let the eye shut on the clenched bunch of nerves
Let the back unwind in lucid repose
Let the mouth widen under night's electric charge
Let the neck relax in the flower of sleep
Let the nostrils flare to the white scent of day
Let the leg stretch from the journey's magnetic force
Let the pubis ignite in the velvet embrace
Let the hip curve in the breeze's grace
Let the ear awaken at the ringing call
Let the hair spread from the skull's wall
Let the chest be lit within the splintered cry
Let the shoulder sleep before the falcon's flight
Let the foot lose its way in the sorcery of time
Let the throat darken with the syllable of space

THE CHILD IS FATHER OF THE MAN

No sé cómo buscarte dentro de mí,
niño que fui: si debo escarbar
encarnizadamente
en la memoria
o invocarte por medio de magias repentinas
en las que no creo.

Estás perdido pero no para ti mismo:
sólo para mí. Sin embargo soy tú,
o eso me dicen quienes parecen
saber más de mí que yo mismo; o que tú.

En el tiempo de la vida
tuviste un tiempo propio,
largo, dilatado
hasta el confín de juegos infinitos.

Sé que jugabas como ahora yo juego:
pero eso no es encontrarte. Soy tu repetición
—siquiera en el esplendor mínimo
del juego— y sus inocencias y sus culpas.

William Wordsworth afirma
que eres mi padre:
él juega un juego estrafalario
con los años, con las edades
y con la genética. Por las entrañas
y por la biología,
mi padre fue otro
—y ya está muerto. Tú estás vivo.
Y es cierto que vives
como una sombra palpitante
dentro de mí. Pero no conozco ese «dentro».

THE CHILD IS FATHER OF THE MAN

I don't know how to seek you out inside me –
child that I was: whether I have to scrape
with gritted nails
in memory's plot
or call you forth with drastic invocations
I don't believe in.

You're lost – not lost to yourself:
only to me. But all the same I'm you,
or so they say, the ones who seem to know
more about me than I do, or than you do.

In the time that's given to a life
you had your own time,
wide and stretching out as far as
the edge, the margin of endless play.

I know you played once as I'm playing now:
but this isn't to meet you. I'm your repetition
– if only in the curtailed splendour
of the game, its guilt and innocence.

Wordsworth declares that you're my father:
himself playing a weird and wild game
with the years, succession
and genetics. For my assembled parts,
the biological thing,
I had another father
– and now he's dead. But you're alive.
No doubt about it – you're alive
like a pulsing shadow
inside me. Yet I have no knowledge of this 'inside'.

Cuando examino el interior de lo que soy
hallo solamente un amasijo de formas
indistintas, apenas discernible
por un esfuerzo del recuerdo.
Pero estás ahí, impalpable, invisible.

Acércate. Pienso a veces
que no quieres hacerlo
para que yo no te mate. O te me escapas
minuciosamente
por una voluntad incomprensible
de ocultamiento. Pues sospecho
que no me tienes miedo
—como no le tiene miedo la sombra
al cuerpo que la proyecta sobre la pared.

Es posible que siempre estés aquí
y seas la forma sagrada
de una ignorancia cósmica
que debería atormentarme.
Pero quizá, mejor aun,
tienes la hondura de una sabiduría
visionaria.

Sin embargo, sé que aborreces
tales grandes palabras, acaso
porque las desconocías
o porque ellas te desconocían.

Entre mil otras cosas, puedo entender
que eres precisamente eso:
el desconocimiento de las grandes palabras.

When I examine the interior of what I am
I find a mass of inchoate forms
that even by an effort of memory
are barely distinguishable.
But you are there – untouchable, invisible.

Come closer. I sometimes think
you don't want to
for fear I'll kill you. Or that deftly
you elude me
out of an unfathomable
will to hide. Then I suspect
you have no fear of me –
as the shadow has no fear of the body
that casts it on the wall.
It could be that you're always here
and that you're the sacred form
of a cosmic ignorance
that should torment me.
Though perhaps, better still,
you've sounded the depths of visionary wisdom.

All the same, I know you hate
such big words, maybe
because you've no knowledge of them
nor they of you.

Among countless other things you may be,
I can understand that you're precisely this:
the ignorance of big words.

Que por el tiempo presente de tu ausencia
o de tu estilo de esconderte
eso me baste. Mientras tanto, en sueños,

murmuro tus cantos sin significado
y en la vigilia intento ponerlos
en líneas irregulares de juego serio,
ese otro confín.

That for the present moment of your absence
or of your manner of hiding
this is enough for me. In the meantime, in dreams,

I croon your songs without meaning
and, awake, I try to place them
in the irregular lines of serious play,
this other edge, this margin.